C000065210

A BOOT UP

BRISTOL

Rodney Legg

First published in Great Britain in 2010

British Library Cataloguing-in-Publication Data
A CIP record for this title is available from the British Library

ISBN 978 1 906887 85 8

PiXZ Books
Halsgrove House, Ryelands Industrial Estate,
Bagley Road, Wellington, Somerset TA21 9PZ
Tel: 01823 653777
Fax: 01823 216796
email: sales@halsgrove.com

An imprint of Halstar Ltd, part of the Halsgrove group of companies
Information on all Halsgrove titles is available at: www.halsgrove.com

Printed and bound in China by Toppan Leefung Printing Ltd

Contents

	How to use this book	4
1	**Northwick and Aust**	7
2	**Siston and the Community Forest**	11
3	**Blaise Castle and Kings Weston Hill**	17
4	**The Harbour and Cabot Tower**	23
5	**Clifton and Sea Mills**	29
6	**Abbots Leigh and Ashton Park**	35
7	**Lower Failand and Easton-in-Gordano**	41
8	**Wraxall and Tyntesfield**	47
9	**Brockley and Chelvey**	53
10	**Stanton Drew and Pensford**	59

How to use this book

The Area

Dramatically poised on the edge of the Avon Gorge, the city of Bristol incorporates its own walking country. Wild walks and country walks begin from Clifton and Henbury. Clifton Suspension Bridge links both with genteel Ashton Park and the virtual jungle of Leigh Woods on the other side. There is also a rich and romantic strand of maritime history from Romans at Sea Mills to Brunel's steamship SS *Great Britain* back home in the dock where she was built.

Bristol was England's second city, after London and has much about it that is like London looked until the Second World War. It was overtaken in the Industrial Revolution, firstly by Birmingham, and then Liverpool when ocean-going liners needed a deep-water port.

Ten selected walks, in circuits of varying lengths, tackle very different terrain. They also explore the city's setting, just beyond the urban sprawl, where you can escape into a very different world. Rocky chasms fringe the Mendip Hills. On the other side of the great conurbation are the Bristol Channel marshes, between the motorways and below the two Severn Bridges. Bristol abounds in engineering works on the grand scale.

The practical route-master approach, with easy to follow descriptions and maps, is laced here with quirky potted facts about connections and treasures to distract you en route. Photographs likewise are chosen both to capture the feeling and theme of very different walks that bring an element of excitement to the easiest, cheapest, healthiest and most popular national leisure pursuit.

The Routes

All routes are circular - meaning they bring you back to the starting point - and are of moderate length. They vary from four to seven miles and are graded from one to three boots - from easy to the more challenging. They are ideal for families or groups of friends looking for an afternoon in historic and scenic settings. There are usually opportunities to pause at a pub or refreshment spot en route. Little of the terrain is pushchair friendly, so back-pack the toddler.

Starting points are given with map references and postcodes. The latter are needed for car-borne navigation systems.

Direction details specify compass points which, clockwise, are N (north), NNE (north-northeast), NE (northeast), ENE (east-northeast), E (east), ESE (east-southeast), SE (south-east), SSE (south-southeast), S (south), SSW (south-southwest), SW (south-west), WSW (west-southwest), W (west), WNW (west-northwest), NW (northwest) and NNW (north-northwest). The general direction can be assumed

to remain the same until another compass point is given. Carry a compass.

Routes are along public rights of way or across access land. Both categories may be subject to change or diversion. Remember that conditions under foot will vary greatly according to the season and the weather. Even urban paths can be muddy.

Parking spaces are specified on the assumption that many walkers will arrive by car or bicycle. Where public transport is mentioned, there were options currently available, but check these with the provider before setting off. Ensure you find out the time of the last bus or train.

Maps

Though we give a self-contained potted description of each walk you may need

a map or global positioning system to find its parking point. Our sketch maps can only be a rough guide. A detailed map will prove useful if you stray away from the route or have to cut the walk short. Phillip's Street Atlas (Bristol & Bath) is excellent.

Bristol, as far as the Ordnance Survey is concerned, is covered by two large-scale sheets. Most of the city, with its northern, eastern and southern surroundings, appears on Explorer Map 155 (Bristol & Bath). For the Bristol Channel and its hinterland see Explorer 154 (Bristol West & Portishead). Access www.ordnancesurvey.co.uk/leisure for availability.

Key to Symbols Used

Level of difficulty:

Easy 🥾

Fair 🥾🥾

More challenging 🥾🥾🥾

Map symbols:

🚗 Park & start

🚻 WC

Tarred Road

----- Footpath

■ Building / Town

🍺 Pub

▲ Landmark

✚ Church

▓▓▓▓ Railway Line

River or Stream

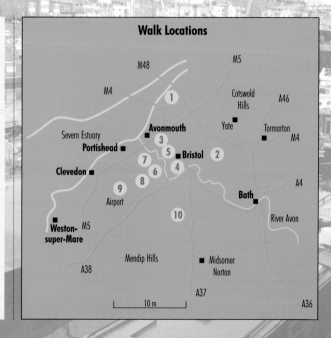

Walk Locations

M48

M5

M4

Cotswold Hills

A46

①

Yate

Severn Estuary

Avonmouth

Tormarton

M4

Portishead

③

⑤ ■**Bristol**

②

Clevedon ■

⑦

④

A4

⑧

⑥

⑨

②

Airport

⑩

Bath

River Avon

Weston-super-Mare

M5

Mendip Hills

■ Midsomer Norton

A38

A37

A4

├─── 10 m

A36

1 Northwick and Aust

A 7-mile circuit in which the country walking is framed by two great modern bridges

Past and present links between England and Wales comprise two former passage points and two great suspension bridges. There is also an almost hidden connection, running south of Northwick and Pilning, which was dug by Victorian navvies for the Great Western Railway. After entering the portals of the Severn Tunnel - imperial length 4 miles 628 yards - the next station beyond Severn Tunnel Junction is Newport, just after the sidings to the steel-works at Llanwern. Its chimneys across the water are the principal industrial landmarks of this walk which is otherwise dominated by the architecture of engineering and transportation in the coast and countryside between the two bridges. The remarkable geology of Aust Cliff is

Level: ♥ ♥
Length: 7 miles
Terrain: Low-lying, liable to muddy patches, and rhyne-crossing diversions.
Park and Start: Turn east from the A403 to Northwick for roadside parking in the vicinity of 1842-dated Sandford's Charity School and Church Farm.
Start ref.: ST 559 867
Postcode: BS35 4HE
Public transport: Buses from Severnside to Thornbury.
Websites: www.boarsheadpub.co.uk
www.severnbridgesvisitorcentre.org.uk

distinctive for its lack of colour co-ordination. The clays, limestones and sands of the Westbury beds come in three distinct shades - dull reddish-brown, bright turquoise and gleaming white.

Map labels:

First Severn Bridge · M48
Aust Cliff
Aust Ferry · 7 · 8 · ✚ ■ Aust
■ Old
6 · Passage · 9
5
Cake Pill
Gout
10 · Lord's
Rhine
Severn Estuary
Second Severn Bridge · 4 · North Worthy Farm · Northwick · 1 · Pilning Road
3a · ■ · 2
Rifle Range · 3
Redwick ■ · M5

① Set off across **Pilning Road** (SW) to the drive through **Northwick Farm**. In 100 metres, in the paddock beyond the buildings, the public path brings us to a stile midway along the right-hand side. Turn left on the other side and follow the hedge to stiles beside the road in 200 metres.

② Turn left (S), along the roadside path, for 250 metres. Turn right (W) at the drive to **North Worthy Farm**, at the start of the slope that rises towards the bridge, and go through the left-hand of the gates. Keep the garden to your right as you cross meadows towards the left-hand side of the second Severn Bridge. Go through the gate in 250 metres and proceed straight ahead in

Severn Lodge - former ferry hostelry

this field which has two public paths. Follow the left-hand hedgerow (SW) for 200 metres.

③ In the next field - providing the red flag is not flying - follow the right-hand hedgerow and then cross the grass to an embankment in 300 metres. Turn left along it and pass to the left of a house in 150 metres. Follow the red and white dan-

ger poles and keep the military **Rifle Range** to your right. The path heads towards Wales (NW) for 500 metres. Across to the left are Redwick and New Passage. **Severn Lodge Farm**, looking out over Red Ledge and Goblin Ledge, used to be a hostelry where travellers waited for the tide.

(3a) Should the red flags be flying you must turn right (NNW) on approaching the red and white poles and follow them to the sentry box beside the estuary.

(4) Whichever way, turn right (NE) on joining the coastal footpath, which is the Severn Way. Seaside marshes and mud-flats of **Sugarhole Sand** and **Northwick Oaze** are across to the left. The **Severn Estuary** begins between 300 and 700 metres away depending on the state of the tide. Extreme tidal phases, caused by the estuary acting like a funnel, bring a rise and fall of 42 feet. **Northwick Warth** is now backed by the man-made rising ground of Northwick Landfill Site.

Bizarre colours on Aust Cliff

(5) In 2,750 metres we reach the road at **Cake Pill Gout**. Turn left (NW) to the corner in 150 metres. Turn right (NE), across a stile, and follow a bank, with a hedge to the right. Cross the stiles and pastures and then climb a ridge in 800 metres. Here there is a second footpath, striking off to the left (N) beside the **Old Passage House** and **Dower House**, following hedges - or way-marks if these are in place - to the road in 400 metres.

A single monstrous pylon, offshore from former Aust Passage, carries the National Grid from Gloucestershire to the Forest of Dean.

(6) Cross it and walk down (SW) to the gap above the **Barns**. Descend to the gates and turnstile of the former **Aust Ferry** in 50 metres. Turn right (N), along the raised concrete road, which goes as far as the **National Grid Jetty** in 500 metres. This is an optional diversion, for the sensation of looking up to the colossal first **Severn Bridge**, which is awesome as it rises on immense concrete piles from Aust Rock and offshore Great Ulverstone. Take care if you walk along the crumbling undercliff of **Aust Cliff** which has multi-coloured layers of clay, limestone and sand with beds of fossils and crushed mussels.

Northwick Church tower

7 On returning to Aust Ferry we turn left (NE), uphill, to **Cliff Farm** and **St Augustine's Vineyard** which is beside the **Old Parsonage**. In 500 metres we pass under the National Grid beside a particularly hideous pylon. Then in another 200 metres, after **Newhouse Farm** and **Changeways**, we come to the back entrance to **Severn View Services**.

8 Turn right here (E), down a leafy track, for 125 metres. Then cross the main road into **Aust** village. **Church Farm** is beside the **Chapelry of St John**. Proceed for 500 metres to the junction with Sandy Lane, between the 1896-dated **Zion Chapel** - now the Evangelical Church - and the ancient **Boar's Head** hostelry.

9 Opposite the Boar's Head, we turn (SW) into a raised droveway beside the **Foss Ditch**. This is signed as the Pilgrim's Way. Proceed straight ahead at a junction with another drove in 600 metres. In another 600 metres we fork right through a gate and cross two fields, for 500 metres, to the right of **Asnum Copse**

10 Cross **Lord's Rhine** and continue straight ahead across the meadows beside **Bilsham Rhine** to return to **Northwick**, via the solitary tower of its former parish church, in 1,500 metres.

The first Severn Bridge (originally the M4 but now the M48 to Chepstow), from Aust Cliff, was built in 1966 with a carriageway 50 feet above the water that is suspended from twin towers of steel rising 521 feet into the air.

First Severn Bridge

2 Siston and the Community Forest

A 4- mile stroll around ancient parkland and newly-planted woods

Mediaeval and Elizabethan Siston Court and ancient St Anne's Church stand on a ridge which marks the first step in the foothills of the Cotswolds. There is a sacred spring, St Anne's Well, beside the road down from the church. This parkland parish also retains stretches of common grassland and a scatter of old woodlands. Their contribution to public access is now being boosted by a jig-saw of new woods that have been created through the Community Forest project. Against all the odds, this green wedge looks like part of Gloucestershire rather than an adjunct to Bristol. In terms of distance, how-ever, it is the proverbial stone's throw away.

Map labels: 13, 14, 12 Siston Court, Siston, 1 Cowleaze Farm, 11 Hanging Wood, Mill Farm, Myrtle Farm, 9, Siston Brook, Fir Tree Lodge, 2, Barns, Blue Lodge, 10, 5, 8, 7, 6, Webb's Heath, 4, 3

Level:
Length: 4 miles
Terrain: Mostly grassy paths, and the one proper hill is downwards, but prepare for a few muddy paddocks.
Park and Start: In Siston, midway between Warmley and Pucklechurch, by turning into the no through road beside St Anne's Church and then turning immediately left into its car-park.
Start ref.: ST 688 753
Postcode: BS16 9LR
Public transport: Buses from Warmley to Pucklechurch.
Websites: www.british-towns.net
www.forestofavon.org.uk

Alpacas at Cowleaze

1 Set off into the lane (S) and turn left (E) away from the main road. Turn right at the corner in 200 metres and then left in 5 metres, through the gate piers of **Cowleaze Farm** and Avon Alpacas. Bear right (SSE) in 50 metres, beside a hedge,

and go through a kissing gate. Follow the power lines uphill beside the paddocks, through a second kissing gate, and continue following the same hedgerow.

2 Leave the power lines in the corner of the field in 800 metres and go over an enormous stone stile. Pass the barns of **Overscourt Farm** in 400 metres, cross a stile beside a gate, and follow the hedgerow to the lane in 100 metres.

3 Turn left, for 30 metres, and then turn right (W) across a stile. Follow the wall behind **Blue Lodge** and then a hedgerow into the pastures. Turn right and then left in the corner of the field in 300 metres and now keep the hedge to your left. Cross the stile in 200 metres and descend towards the pylons and the city. The next stile is in the left-hand corner of the slope in 200 metres. Go under the power cables, to a stile in a further 200 metres.

Dating from 1090, the highly-decorated lead font in Siston Church is one of six from the same mould, out of a total of 38 such rare fonts in England.

4 Bear right, diagonally across the pasture, to a steel gate. A stub-end of green lane leads to sheds and smallholdings beside the main road in 400 metres.

Edwardian-period members of the Rawlins family from Siston Court feature in the chancel-arch wall murals in Siston Church.

Historic stone stile

Siston village

5 Cross **Siston Lane**, from **Fir Tree Lodge**, into **Webb's Heath** common land and follow the hedge straight ahead. Cross the next road to the gates, in 200 metres.

6 Cross the stile in 150 metres and go straight across the paddock, to a stile in the opposite fence in 200 metres. **Moulds Court Farm** is up to your right. Descend in the pasture, following the hedge, and cross a stile in 200 metres. Then the hedgerow path crosses the **Siston Brook** in 150 metres.

7 Turn right beside the pond in 50 metres, through the kissing gate, and then left. Cross a stile in the top left-hand corner of the pasture in 175 metres.

Siston Brook

Siston Court was rebuilt by Sir Walter Dennys in Elizabethan times and remained in the family for many generations.

8 Turn right (N) and follow the hedgerow, to a junction of paths, in 175 metres. Turn right (NE), through a kissing gate, and go down across the pasture to a stile to the left of the gate above the buildings of **Brook Farm** in 250 metres. Go up the slope to the stile opposite **Myrtle Farm** entrance in 150 metres.

9 Turn right (SE), keeping to the roadside verge for 150 metres, to re-cross the brook on the bend.

Noises off may include the evocative whistle of the steam locomotive from Avon Valley Railway at Bitton.

10 Turn left (NE) along the drive to **Mill Farm** in 400 metres. Fork right (E) on its green. Follow the stream over two fields and go under the power lines. Having entered the third field, in 400 metres, we bear left (NE) - diagonally across it - up into the top-right hand corner in 300 metres.

11 Turn right and then left (N), to enter the path uphill through the western extremity of **Hanging Wood**. In 75 metres, on entering a grassy slope, follow the hedgerow up and over the hill. Bear right on top (NE), following the glade, heading for a point to the left of the imposing lines of **Siston Court** in 500 metres.

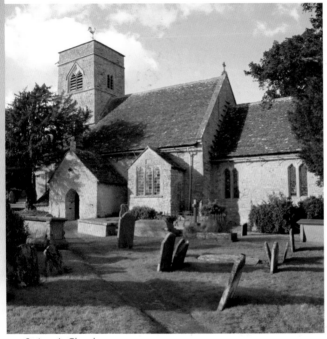

St Anne's Church

12 Exit from the open space across a stile and turn left (N) through a belt of woodland. Turn right in the field, in 50 metres, beside the duck pond, to the barns in 250 metres.

13 Follow the track (E) for 200 metres, then turn right (SSE), to cross the old stone wall and pass the hexagonal dovecote. Go over the stone stile in the corner in 100 metres and turn left (E) along the drive. Follow the footpath signs to the road in 200 metres.

14 Turn right (S), making sure you walk single-file towards oncoming traffic, to the gate to the tower of **Siston Church** in 200 metres. The car-park is on the other side of the churchyard in 100 metres.

3 Blaise Castle and Kings Weston Hill

Publicly-owned mansions, follies and woods in a 6-mile hilltop circuit

The original Blaise Castle, surviving in the trees, is an Iron Age hill-fort. Bristol Corporation bought Blaise Castle Estate, with 400 acres of woodland, in 1926 to preserve the hilltop setting of a folly-like mansion with four crenellated towers. It was built in 1771 by Thomas Farr, the Master of the Society of Merchant Venturers, and looks the part, being 'all ship-shape and Bristol fashion'. It became the home of Quaker banker John Scandrett Harford.

In 1809 he commissioned John Nash to turn it into an architectural delight with a picturesque-style thatched dairy and Blaise Hamlet of nine Hobbit-like homes. The corn mill is Stratford Mill from West

Level: 🌿 🌿

Length: 6 miles

Terrain: Muddy in places and quite demanding on the slopes.

Park and start: The car-park for Blaise Castle Estate is beside Kings Weston Road to the west of the house.

Public transport: Buses from the city centre to Kingsweston.

Websites: www.bristol.gov.uk/parks
www.kingswestonhouse.co.uk

Harptree, being dismantled and brought here in 1952, when its original location was flooded for Chew Valley Reservoir. Kingsweston House, the other mansion on the ridge, is a Sir John Vanbrugh extravaganza from 1710. It was created as a gentrified mock-castle.

Blaise
Hamlet ■ 2 ✛ Harford
3
Blaise Castle ■ 1
■ Mill
12
4
Stables 11 8
Kingsweston 7 Kings
House Weston Hill
10 ▲ Mast 6
The Grove 5
9 Coombe
Dingle

17

1 Set off (E) to the toilets, café and **Blaise Castle Museum** in 800 metres. Follow its drive (N) to the main road and turn left and then right, into **Hallen Road**, to the gap in the left-hand wall in 150 metres. Walk around **Blaise Hamlet**.

Norman St Mary's Church at Henbury has a tombstone to Scipio Africanus, the 18-year-old Negro servant of the Earl of Suffolk, who died in 1720.

2 Return to the junction beside **No. 270** - Rose Bank - and turn left (E), to the corner opposite **Blaise Inn** in 150 metres. Cross to **Church Lane** on the corner and turn right (S) into **Church Close** beside the house dated 1624 and named for city merchant Anthony Edmonds. Proceed to **Henbury Church** to see the gravestone to the African slave and pass to the right of the tower into the far part of the churchyard in 150 metres.

Blaise Castle Museum

Henbury slave's grave

Blaise Hamlet

Iron Age Blaise Castle - now with a folly on top - has double banks and ditches on two sides but only needed palisades around the remainder of its seven acres where precipitous hillsides rendered fortifications unnecessary.

Clustering around their village green, chocolate-box John Nash cottages at Blaise Hamlet were built for estate pensioners in 1809, and given to the National Trust in 1943.

Hazel Brook

(3) Exit down the steps and through the tunnel under the wall. The public path re-enters the estate and crosses a stream in 100 metres. Turn right (SW), into the grassy strip, and follow the **Hazel Brook** downstream to **Stratford Mill** in 500 metres. It joins the **River Trim**.

(4) Proceed straight ahead at the cross-roads of paths, continuing to follow the stream, into landscape architect Humphry Repton's drive - and cycleway - down through the wooded gorge. A rocky gorge is up to the right and a steep slope to the left. The cycleway follows the left bank and there is a dirt track - for the adventurous - on the other side of the brook. The two options meet again at a couple of bridges. Continue weaving down the valley to the car-park at **Coombe Dingle** in 2,000 metes.

(5) Turn right (W) up the road which is called **The Dingle**. Turn right (N) in 200 metres, into **The Grove**, and follow it uphill through cosy suburbia for 350 metres. Pass **Pitchcombe Gardens** and **Cedar Court**.

(6) Turn right (E) after **No. 28** into a driveway between hedges and gardens. Pass to the left of the last house, which is **Pennywell**, in 200 metres. Follow the path under a rustic bridge and continue for 50 metres down into the woods.

(7) Turn left (N), up the valley, and bear left in 200 metres, into a grassy slope with houses up to the left. Climb into the wooded hillside, straight ahead, and keep going upwards through the trees to a grassy bank on the summit of **Kings Weston Hill** in 400 metres. The hilltop earthwork encircled an Iron Age settlement.

Iron Age settlement

8 Turn left on top (SW), along the wide grassy strip, which would have commanding views over both Bristol and Severnside if only there were occasional gaps in the tree canopy on each side. In 1,500 metres we pass a communications mast, above a series of old quarries, and proceed along the access road for 400 metres.

9 Cross the bridge (W) over **King's Weston Lane** and enter **Shirehampton Park**. Turn right (N) in 50 metres, and pass to the left of a Gothic folly - very Transylvanian - in a further 50 metres. Drop down the drive and follow the avenue of lime trees to **Kingsweston House**. Turn left in 400 metres, and go up the steps. Around the corner is a delightful **Tea-room** beside the terrace looking across to Severnside and the lower Severn Bridge with the Black Mountains and the Forest of Dean over the water.

10 Turn right (E) to exit along the driveway beside the **Brew House** in 150 metres. Cross into **Napier Miles Road** (NE) and pass Robert Mylne's 1763-dated **Stable Block**.

Water and wind erosion to the natural limestone pavement at Blaise Castle is known as Goram's Footprint for its folklore associations with the legendary giant.

Industrial Severnside

11 Cross **King's Weston Road**, in 500 metres, straight ahead into **Limekiln Wood**. Bear left up through the laurels and continue straight ahead at a woodland cross-roads in 750 metres. In a further 500 metres the main track turns to the right.

12 Here we bear left (N) into the field and then right (E) into 150 metres, into another belt of hilly woodland. This is Iron Age **Blaise Castle** (plus a Gothic folly up in the trees). Turn left (N) in 50 metres, to follow the outer ditch which bends to the right in 100 metres. Follow it for 300 metres, to a gap in the outer rampart, through which a track zig-zags down (N) into the grassland in 100 metres. Cross it to the car-park in 250 metres.

4 The Harbour and Cabot Tower

A 4-mile circuit of the Floating Harbour and the two hills overlooking it

The Brandon Hill landmark, in Gothic mock-Tudor with a spire and globe on top, marks the achievements of Venetian merchant John Cabot and son Sebastian. They sailed from Bristol and reached Newfoundland, Labrador, Hudson's Bay and Maryland. The present Floating Harbour - to name the 80 acres of water with docks and quays - dates from 1809 when the main flow of the Avon was diverted into a 'New Cut' to the south. Imports included casks of port, sherry and claret - the red wine of Bordeaux - plus champagne which first became fizzy when it burst its bottles

Level: 🐾 🐾
Length: 4 miles
Terrain: Asphalt, cobbles and open space incorporating two strenuous hills.
Park & start: In Cumberland Road, on the north side of the River Avon, between the Cottage Inn and River City.
Start ref.: ST 572 722
Postcode: BS1 6XG
Public transport: Inner city buses and harbour ferry.
Websites: www.ssgreatbritain.org.uk
www.stmaryredcliffe.co.uk

on this side of the water. Trade soon evolved into slaves, tobacco, rum and sugar. Isambard Kingdom Brunel built his first two steamships here - with the *Great Britain* being brought home in 1970.

Bristol Marina

1 Set off (N) with your back to the River Avon, into **Mardyke Ferry Road**. Pass Gefle Close and Canada Way and cross Cumberland Close in 150 metres. A footpath leads to the waterside at **Baltic Wharf** in 50 metres.

Brunel's first ship, the 1,230-ton wooden paddle steamer Great Western, was launched near old Prince Street swing-bridge on 19 July 1837.

2 Turn right (E) and skirt **Bristol Marina** in 150 metres, turning left across the slipway beside City of Bristol Rowing Club, and continue to the toilets and chandlery in 100 metres. Pass the theatre scenery workshop in 75 metres and turn left (beside railway track set in the road). Pass the huge **Albion Dock** - currently dry and almost empty - and follow 'Cross Harbour Ferry' signs to **Gasferry Road** in 175 metres.

(3) Turn left (NE), to the entrance to **SS Great Britain** and **Dockyard Café Bar** at **Wapping Wharf**. Turn right (E) to pass the **Maritime Heritage Centre, Brunel's Buttery, Harbour Railway** and the historic steam crane. Continue to the line of large cranes beside the **City History Museum** in 1,000 metres. A 1997-dated plaque, unveiled by Ian White MEP, remembers 'countless African, men, women and children whose enslavement and exploitation brought much prosperity to Bristol'.

(4) Cross **Wapping Road** to **Merchant Quays** and follow the harbour path into and then across **Bathurst Basin** to the **Ostrich Inn** in 200 metres. Turn left, between ancient **Phoenix Wharf** (formerly Alfred Wharf and then King Wharf) and **Red Cliff Caverns**. Sand was removed for ballast and glass-making. Go up **Addercliff Ramp** to **Redcliffe Parade** and the **Colossium** in 250 metres.

The keel of Brunel's second liner, the 2,936-ton iron-plated steamship Great Britain, was laid down on 19 July 1839 and completed in 1843 as the first propeller-driven ocean-going ship in the world.

SS Great Britain

The Ostrich Inn

5 Cross **Redcliffe Hill** to **St Mary Redcliffe** in 100 metres, which to **Queen Elizabeth** was 'the fairest, goodliest, and most famous parish church in England' and had teenage poet Thomas Chatterton's room above the hexagonal north porch.

6 Head for the roundabout and re-cross the road at the pedestrian crossing. Now turn right along the pavement and pass the **Quaker Burial Ground** in 100 metres. Turn left (NW), along **Redcliffe Way**, and cross **Bascule Bridge** in a further 100 metres.

The Arnolfini

7 Turn left into **The Grove** with the **Hole in the Wall** to your right. Cross **Prince Steet** in 300 metres to the **Arnolfini**, **Bush House** and the **Shakespeare Tavern**. Turn right (N) for 75 metres and then left beside the **Bristol Hotel**, into **Farr's Lane**. Cross **Pero's Bridge** from **Narrow Quay** to **Bordeaux Quay** in 150 metres. Turn right (N) to the water-steps below **The Centre** in 200 metres.

8 Turn left (W) and take the second turning on the left, into **College Green** - beside Queen Victoria's statue - between the **Marriott Hotel** and **St Augustine's Parade** in 100 metres. Pass between **Bristol Cathedral** and the **Council House** in 150 metres, into **Deanery Road**.

9 Turn right (N) into **College Street** in 100 metres. Pass the double junctions with **Brandon Street** and **St George's Road** in 150 metres and bear left, uphill from **Dean's Court**. Then turn left (NW), up **Hill Street** in 50 metres.

10 Turn left (SW), up **Great George Street**, in 100 metres. Pass **Georgian House Museum** and **St George's Concert Hall**, and continue upwards to **Queen Charlotte Street** in 150 metres. Turn right, and then left, in 50 metres, into **Brandon Hill** open space and up across the grass to the **Cabot Tower** on the summit in 150 metres.

11 Turn left (SW), down through the trees, towards the harbour. There is a maze of paths but having found steps we descend to the bottom path (aiming for the multi-colour block of flats) in about 250 metres. Turn right and exit through the gates, in the corner of the open space, to drop down to **Jacob's Hill Road**

12 Cross (W) into **Constitution Hill** and proceed uphill, passing Bellevue, Hill View and Clifton Wood Road, to multiple junctions on **Lower Clifton Hill** in 300 metres. Turn left, to pass **Goldney Hall**, and left down **Goldney Avenue** in 50 metres. Turn left immediately (SW), between the college car-park and **No.1**, down narrow **Goldney Lane** footpath.

13 Pass the end of Goldney Road and continue down steps to **Ambra Terrace** in 250 metres. Proceed straight ahead, down **Ambra Vale**, to **Hotwell Road** in 150 metres.

14 Turn right and then left (S), in 50 metres, to cross at the junction from **Holy Trinity Church**, into **Merchants Road**. Pass the **Merchants Arms** and head for the great red blockhouse that was Wills' tobacco warehouse. Cross the **Swing Bridge** between the harbour and **Cumberland Basin** in 300 metres.

15 Pass **Nova Scotia Place**, with its 1811-dated hotel, and bear left (SE) into **Avon Crescent**. This joins **Cumberland Road** in 150 metres. Turn left (E) to return to the **Cottage Inn** and your car in 200 metres.

Cabot Tower

5 Clifton and Sea Mills

*A 6-mile circuit of the northern side
of the Avon Gorge plus Clifton 'village'*

For a dramatic setting, Bristol is up there with Durham and Edinburgh, as the River Avon cuts through a high plateau of carboniferous limestone that was laid down in warm-water seas 330 million years ago. This geophysical divide contributes to a remarkable ecological diversity in which three key plants carry the city's name - Bristol rock-cress, Bristol onion and Bristol whitebeam. The latter, a tree discovered in 1854, sports a multiplicity of sub-species. Dominating all is Clifton Suspension Bridge. On the toplands, at the edge of a grassy limestone plateau, Clifton village contrasts with Bristol proper. Clifton Down and Durdham Down merge as a seamless entity adjacent to Bristol Zoo. This is a Victorian specimen in its own right. The Observatory with its Camera Obscura is another novelty.

Level: ♥ ♥
Length: 6 miles
Terrain: Variable, from steep slopes to level pavments, plus some muddy patches.
Park and start: Approach Clifton up Whiteladies Road, which is the B3129, and cross Clifton Suspension Bridge to park on the Somerset side beside Bridge Road or in North Road.
Start ref.: ST 565 731
Postcode: BS8 3PA
Public transport: Buses from the city centre to Clifton.
Websites: www.at-bristol.org.uk
www.clifton-suspension-bridge.org.uk

Map

Roman building

Sea Mills

7 8 11 Thatched Lodge
9 12 Stoke Bishop
10
Old Sneed Park

Durdham Down

Pitch and Pay Lane

13

Portway

Avon Gorge

5 6
4
3 2

Clifton Down

14

15

16

Zoo
Engineer's House

Clifton Cathedral

Camera Obscura

17

North Road
Bridge Road

1

18 **Clifton Suspension Bridge**

Clifton Village

Avon Gorge and Camera Obscura

kiosk - to head away from urban Clifton. This path passes **The Observatory** (combining the Camera Obscura above and the Giant's Cave below) from where we follow the western bank of an Iron Age fort with the **Avon Gorge** immediately to the left.

Clifton Down and Suspension Bridge

(1) Set off across the **Suspension Bridge** for a stomach-churning antidote to vertigo. The River Avon is 245 feet below. Turn left (N) on the Bristol side of the bridge, by taking the asphalt path beside its outer rails - opposite the

(2) In 400 metres we reach Clifton suburbia, opposite the **Engineers House**. Turn left along the asphalt paths down the slope and through the beech avenue which leads to the cross-roads in 400 metres. Here we cross **Bridge Valley Road** and enter the next section of **Clifton Down**.

3 Turn left (W) in 50 metres to follow a scrubby path between the clearings. Keep going straight ahead, towards the sound of the traffic, until the edge of the Gorge is visible in 200 metres. The path now bears right (NNE). Keep the **River Avon** to the left.

The 20th-century engineering achievement is a network of 75 miles of drainage tunnels from the River Frome at Eastville - across three miles of suburban Bristol - to a 16-feet diameter outfall into the River Avon which was constructed between 1951 and 1962 (to save the city from flash-floods).

Sea Mills

4 In 300 metres the **Circular Road** is to our right. Continue beside it for 500 metres. The road begins to bend to the left after a terrace of houses appears on the skyline at Downleaze.

5 Turn left (NW) across the grass on approaching a pair of boundary stones for 'CD' (Clifton Down) and 'WD' (War Department). In 50 metres we enter the trees and turn left (SW) to descend into a gully. Pass a vertical air-shaft in 125 metres. This ventilates **Clifton Down Tunnel** of the Clifton Extension Railway (which goes to Sea Mills, Avonmouth and Severn Bridge). At the bottom, in 200 metres, we emerge from dense vegetation into a patch of level grass beside the outfall of the **Northern Stormwater Interceptor**. This discharges here into the tidal River Avon.

31

6 Prepare to cross to the other side of the **Portway** when there is a break in the traffic. Do so with alertness and alacrity. The only pavement is beside the Avon. Turn right (NW), downstream, with the river to your left. Join the waterside path in 500 metres.

7 Follow this for 1,750 metres to the inlet beside the **Old Signal Station**. Turn right (NE) to cross over or go under the railway at **Sea Mills Station** in 50 metres. Pass the site of **Roman Abonae** which was a fort, port and settlement. Troops were ferried from here to Cardiff. The great stone walls called the **Roman Harbour** date from an 18th-century whaling station.

8 Proceed straight ahead to go under the road bridge in 150 metres but then turn immediately right (SE), uphill between **Abon House** and its garages. The path emerges in **Roman Way**.

The Camera Obscura, a 'dark chamber' combination of a lens and mirror installed by William West in 1828, projects a real-time image of the Suspension Bridge and Clifton Down on to a white-painted copper dish five feet in diameter.

9 Turn right (SW), to the foundations of a Roman building on the island at the junction in 200 metres. Turn uphill beside it (SSW), along **Horse Shoe Drive** which runs parallel to the main road. Continue to the end of the road in 300 metres where a public path descends steps to the Portway.

Roman building

10 Turn left from this short path, into the trees, and keep the railway down to your right. You join the main path (E) through the woodland of **Old Sneed Park** nature reserve. Bear right on approaching a stone wall with houses above and join a track above the lake in 350 metres. Turn left (N), uphill, to **Glenavon Park** in 200 metres.

11 Turn right (NE), to the corner in 100 metres. Turn right (SE), to the junction with **Old Sneed Park** - the road this time - in 150 metres.

12 Turn left (NE) and cross **Mariners Drive** in 100 metres. Immediately turn right (SE), opposite the thatched **Lodge**, into a

footpath which follows an old stone wall uphill to **St Mary Magdalene Church** in **Sneyd Park** in 300 metres. Continue straight ahead, between the butressed chimney of **Woodlands Lodge** and an active badger set. Cross **Church Road** , in 175 metres and continue uphill beside the toll-bar on the back wall of **Pitch and Pay Cottage**. The path becomes **Pitch and Pay Lane** which brings us to the **Circular Road** in 600 metres.

Clifton

The Giant's Cave, otherwise known as Ghyston from one of Bristol's mythical supernatural creatures, is thought to have been the hermit's chapel that gave its name to St Vincent's Rocks.

13 Cross into **Durdham Down** open space. Bear left (E) and head for buildings to the right of the Water Tower. Cross **Ladies Mile** road in 400 metres. Then in 300 metres, we reach **Upper Belgrave Road**.

14 Turn right (S) into **Clifton**. Scrubby ground hides traces of extensive Romano-British lead workings. The Roman road from Sea Mills to Bath ran close by. Keep grassland to your right for 500 metres.

15 Turn left (SE) down **The Avenue** on approaching **Bristol Zoo**. Turn left (NE) at the end, in 350 metres, into **Guthrie Road**. In the field to the right of the church - now turned into flats - A. E. J. Collins scored the highest recorded innings in the history of cricket (628 not out, in a junior house match, in June 1899).

16 Turn right (SE) in 100 metres, into **Pembroke Road**, and follow it for 400 metres. Pass **All Saints' Church** and turn right into **Pembroke Vale**. Turn right and then left (S) in 250 metres, beside the airport-modern lines of **Clifton Cathedral**, into **Clifton Park** in another 50 metres.

17 Turn right (SW) at the cross-roads in 200 metres, beside **Vyvyan House**, up the next stretch of **Clifton Park**. Cross to the opposite pavement, over the pedestrian crossing beside **Clifton High School**, and walk up to **Christ Church** and the grassland beyond in 400 metres. Bear left (S) after crossing **Clifton Down Road**, from **Harley Place**, across the park to **The Mall** and **Royal Oak** in 150 metres.

18 Turn right (W) in 50 metres, along cobbled **Gloucester Street**, to the **Grapes Tavern** and **Coronation Tap** in 250 metres. Turn right, beside **Bridge House**, and then left. Pass **Sion Court** and **Sion Lane**. Then cross the grass to return to **Clifton Suspension Bridge** in 200 metres.

Human fly

6 Abbots Leigh and Ashton Park

A 7-mile circuit from Bristol's parkland descends to the Avon Walkway below Clifton Suspension Bridge

The feudal landscape beside Avon Gorge was granted to the Ashton family by Richard II. Ashton Park, its 850 acres grazed by fallow deer, then became home to the Smyth family. They built the Inigo Jones mansion, created the 18th-century parkland, and remained in residence for 400 years. Sir John Henry Greville Smyth died without leaving an heir. His 15,000-acre holdings were auctioned in 1915. The special 850 acres of secret heartlands behind the wall were acquired by Bristol City Council in the Second World War. Adjoining to the north is Abbots Leigh

Level: 🥾 🥾
Length: 7 miles
Terrain: Mainly parkland and woodland paths with a couple of reasonably gradual slopes.
Park & start: Turn from the A369 at the George Inn, Abbots Leigh, into Church Road and park outside Leigh Lodge, opposite the Village Hall.
Start ref.: ST 542 737
Postcode: BS8 3QU
Public transport: Buses from Bristol to Portishead.
Websites: www.abbotsleigh.org.uk
www.ashtoncourtestate.co.uk

which was a manor of mediaeval Bristol Abbey. The delightful Abbot's Pond would have provided the monks' fish dish on Fridays.

(map labels) Abbots Leigh · The Priory · 1 · 2 · 13 · 15 · 12 · 14 · Stokeleigh · 3 · Nightingale Valley · 4 · 5 · Abbot's Pool · Avon Gorge · 11 · 7 · Clifton Lodge Gate · Fifty Acre Wood · 8 · Ashton Court Estate · Ashton Park · 10 · Longwood Lane · 9 · 6

1. Set off along **Church Road** (NE), passing 1879-dated cottages and **Chantry House**, to **Holy Trinity Church** in 500 metres. Turn right (SE) opposite the church, immediately after **Avonhurst**, and walk down across the children's playground (donated by Mrs R. J. Fry in 1925). Head into a hillside pasture terraced with lynchets and also continue straight ahead across the next field to the gate and stile in 500 metres.

2. Cross the drive to the gate and stile on the other side. Follow the left-hand hedge and then turn right, beside a fence, to the centre part of the drive from the roadside lodge into Leigh Woods, in 700 metres.

Hotwells

3. Cross the drive to the gate and stile to the left of **Stokeleigh** bungalow. Bear right in the field, diagonally, to the far corner between the chalet and a dormer bungalow in 300 metres. Follow the drive to the main road in 125 metres.

4. Turn left, downhill through the traffic lights, and then left (E) into **North Road** in 200 metres. Turn left in 200 metres, opposite **Valley View**, and then immediately right to follow the lowest of the footpath options, down through **Nightingale Valley** to the railway bridge and Avon Walkway in 800 metres. The woods were given to the National Trust by Sir George Wills in 1909.

5 Turn right (S), along the track beside the tidal reed-beds of the **River Avon**, and pass beneath **Clifton Suspension Bridge** in 250 metres. You find yourself opposite the entrance to Clifton Rocks Railway and the great timber wharves of Hotwells.

6 Turn right at a bridge in 750 metres, to re-cross the railway, with a view of Cumberland Basin down to the left. Then cross the main road, in 35 metres, to the safety of its opposite pavement. Turn right (NW) along it and climb **Rownham Hill** into **Leighwoods** suburb in 800 metres.

A compulsive and copious creator of church embroidery, Janet Fry produced hundreds of altar fronts and ecclesiastical banners, and married her cousin Roderick Fry in 1889.

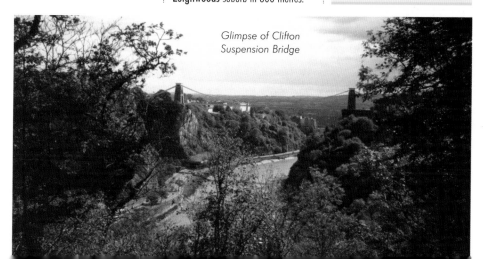

Glimpse of Clifton Suspension Bridge

Ashton Park

(7) Turn left (SW) through **Clifton Lodge Gate** into **Ashton Court Estate** and follow the **Lime Avenue**. This is **Ashton Park**. Continue straight ahead in 400 metres at the junction with the golf course access road. Then in 150 metres turn right (W) into an unpaved track - with your back to the City Centre - and head to the woods above **Redwood Avenue**. The golf course is across to the right and Ashton Court down to the left.

(8) Bear left in 300 metres and follow the cycleway into the wood. Proceed straight ahead, following signs for the Avon Timberland Trail, for the entirety of the main track through the wood. This follows its top edge with steep slopes dropping down to the left.

(9) In 2,000 metres, at the far end of the wood, we come to **Longwood Lane**. Turn right (N), opposite the quarry entrance, and walk uphill beside the park wall to the **Old Bristolians' Playing Field** (defended by gun embrasures from Second World War anti-invasion defences).

(10) Cross **Beggar Bush Lane**, in 700 metres, downhill into **Weir Lane**. Turn right (NE) in 200 metres, into **Fifty Acre Wood**, and bear left. Follow access arrows through the wood to its far left-hand end, in 1,000 metres, and exit across a stile.

11 Turn left (NW), downhill towards the orchard, and cross **Manor Road** in 250 metres. Enter **Fish Pond Wood** in 100 metres. This is managed as a nature reserve by North Somerset Council. Pass **Abbot's Pool** in 300 metres. Continue straight ahead beyond the pond for 100 metres.

Abbot's Pool

Abbots Leigh pantiles

12 Turn right on reaching the garden hedge. Descend rocky steps and cross a stone bridge. The enhancement project by Walter Melville Wills is from the 1920s. Follow the wall up to **Bosley** and **Lane End** in 400 metres.

13 Bear left after **Abbotsway** in 300 metres and cross the lane in 25 metres. Continue straight ahead on the other side, for 100 metres, to the road beside **The Beeches**.

Gothic Priory in Manor Road

15 Proceed to **Pill Road**, beside the **George Inn**, in 600 metres. The parish's original Church House, this was rented by churchwardens as a hostelry, from about 1740. Church Road is opposite.

Emerge from the forest canopy to a breathtaking view of Clifton Suspension Bridge and pass underneath Isambard Kingdom Brunel's ultimate engineering feat which was completed as his memorial.

14 Turn left (NE), along **Manor Road**, and pass **Abbots Leigh Nursing Home** (in the former **Manor House** home of the Trenchards and a succession of Bristol merchants). Then pass **The Priory** which was built in flamboyant early Gothic style by Bristol lead importer Christopher George in 1831. Its view is over Abbotsleigh Cottages and Royal Portbury Dock to South Wales.

7 Lower Failand and Easton-in-Gordano

*A 7-mile circuit overlooking the Severn Estuary
with the M5 cleverly landscaped out of sight*

Bristol's 'Chocolate Country' became the core of the city's southern green belt through the foresight of the Fry family of Failand House, who donated their 363 acres to the National Trust in 1944. The gift, from Miss Agnes Fox, was in memory of Sir Edward and Lady Fry. Planning law was effectively shelved for the Second World War but post-war development was already in prospect, and land in the centre of Failand had already become a housing estate. This Trust-owned wedge of fields and woods still holds the urban line where it touches the back gardens of bungalows opposite Rudgleigh Inn at Easton-in-Gordano. The western slopes overlook Portishead, Royal Portbury Docks, and the Avon Bridge.

Level: ♥ ♥
Length: 7 miles
Terrain: Gentle paths but liable to be muddy in places.
Park & start: From Sandy Lane in the layby beside St Bartholomew's Church at Lower Failand.
Start ref.: ST 515 735
Postcode: BS8 3SR
Public transport: Buses from Bristol to Portishead.
Websites: www.easton-in-gordano.org.uk
www.maps.google.co.uk

41

Lower Failand, in the parish of Wraxall, was given a prim Gothic church by Richard Vaughan of Elms Lea, Bath, in a lavish building project from 1883 to 1887.

1 Set off downhill (SW), passing **The Chantry** and **Red Roofs**, followed by the 1839-built **Old School**. Proceed straight ahead at the junction, in 300 metres, up **Horse Race Lane**.

St Bartholomew's Church seats 300 people and has a 120-feet spire that acts as a focal point in this undulating landscape.

2 Turn right (N) between the houses in 75 metres. Turn left (W) in 30 metres, into the back lane, from **Hill View Farm**. On reaching the stables at the end of the lane, in 200 metres, turn left (S) across the stiles and paddocks. Bear right in the field (SW), after the hedge in 200 metres, across to a hunting gate into the **New Forest** in 200 metres, and about the same distance from the left-hand end of the wood.

3) Proceed straight ahead into the trees and then bear right up the slope, and down beside the fence across a field-sized clearing in 350 metres. Continue down through the next section of woodland, in 100 metres, to **Portbury Road**, and emerge from the older trees beside a disused quarry in 200 metres.

4) Turn left (S) up the road. Face the oncoming traffic. Turn right in 200 metres (W) along the drive beside **Limekiln Cottage** to **Higher Farm** barn conversions in 300 metres.

The distant skyline ripples along the cloud-line from the Black Mountains above Abergavenny to the Forest of Dean beyond Chepstow.

5) Go through the gate on the other side of the former farm-yard into a double-fenced track to **Breach Wood** in 300 metres. In a further 250 metres we reach **Charlton Drive**, opposite the school. Turn right (N) to the bend in 200 metres.

6) Here we turn right, through the trees, to a gate into the field in 50 metres. Cross this diago-nally (NE), down the slope, to the far lower corner in 350 metres. Ignore a second path which branches off to the left to an iron turnstile set in the hedge. Our path exits at the gate and then crosses an arable field, to a stile into the scrub on the other side, in another 350 metres.

7) Here the path follows a gully and passes an old privy in 200 metres. We then walk beside ruined cottages, in an idyllic setting in their own sheltered valley, and follow the drive down to the road in 300 metres. Cross with caution, to the stile beside the gate on the other side, and climb the slope (E). Look out for wild-fowl rising from the lake to the left.

8) Turn left (NE) in 75 metres, along the farm road, and then leave it to proceed straight ahead from the stile and gate. Follow the woodland fence up and over **Windmill Hill**. Cross the stiles in 200 metres and continue into the corner of this field, in 250 metres, where we cross a stile into **Budding's Wood**. Proceed straight ahead at the cross-

roads of paths in the wood and descend to a stile into the field, in 250 metres, for a panoramic view of the upper Bristol Channel with South Wales in the background. Honor Farm is the distinctive building in the foreground.

There are few glimpses of nearby Bristol, apart from its outer tower blocks, and for the most part the countryside is as rural as any in Somerset.

9 Our onward route bears a little inland, down to a stub-end of scrubby green lane between the oak trees in 100 metres, to **Failand Lane** in 150 metres. Cross the stile beside the gate and bear left (N) up and over the rise to a stile to the right of the gate and Honor Farm in 100 metres.

10 Join **Coombe Lane** and proceed straight ahead towards the wooded hills. **Summer House Wood**, to the right, is the northern extremity of the National Trust's Failand Estate. The road becomes a green lane in 300 metres and we continue along it (NE) to the stream-side wood in a further 300 metres.

Rudgleigh Inn

11 Turn right, across the stile, into the field, and then turn left (N) to follow the stream. Turn left, across a stile into the wood, in 100 metres. In 200 metres we turn right (NE) and climb the slope. Skirt to the left of any fallen trees. In 100 metres this woodland track brings us to a stile at the top.

12 Cross the field to the next stile, in 100 metres, with a view of the M5 and its Avon Bridge crossing to the left. Bear left in the next field, following the hedge down towards the traffic, to stiles to the right of the barn in 200 metres.

13 This is **Easton-in-Gordano**. Turn right (SE), along the roadside path, to **Rudgleigh Inn** on the hill in 250 metres. Here we turn right, into the narrower of the two openings opposite the public house, which is beside **Rudgleigh Cottages**. In 100 metres we enter National Trust land, to the left of **Topsview**, and continue straight ahead across two fields, to **Happerton Lane**, in 450 metres.

The big surprise is the absence of sight and sound from the closest length of the M5 - just a mile away - as it has been tucked away out of view on the far side of a wooded precipice.

Avon Bridge

14 Turn left (E), down the road, for 300 metres. The pebbled red sandstone walls of Happerton Farm bring us to its 1614-dated walls and windows which look distinctly ex-Bath Abbey. Turn right at the junction to continue along Happerton Lane for a further 200 metres.

15 Turn right (S) to **Upper Happerton Farm** and follow its drive for 200 metres. Then bear left, following the hedge to a gate and stile, into the field straight ahead. Keep the farm to your right. Bear right in the field, to a gate and stile midway along the right-hand fences, in 125 metres. Then turn left, up the slope, to another gate and stile on the skyline in 100 metres.

16 From here we bear right (SW) with **Leigh Wood** down to the left. We are back on National Trust land for virtually the remainder of the walk. Glance back for a widening panorama of the Severn Estuary and its bridges. Follow the woodland fence (SSW) for 600 metres, to cross a footbridge, and climb steps to a field with a view of the valley and woods. Proceed straight ahead across this pasture, to the stile in the middle of the hedgerow - to the right of a cattle-trough - in 200 metres.

17 Turn left (SE) along **Sandy Lane**. Pass the first houses, then **Boundary House**, to descend to **Mulberry Farm** in 400 metres (with its mulberry tree in the roadside

corner). Just beyond it we turn right (SW) between the field gate and **Markham Book**.

18 The far end of this field, in 250 metres, brings us to a gate into **West Tanpit Wood**. In a further 250 metres, on reaching the remains of an old wall, we turn right (NW) to climb the hill. Pass a stone for 'Hathway's Boundary 1775'.

1614-dated Happerton Farm

19 From the top of the slope, in 200 metres, we cross a stile into a field and bear right (W) to follow the fence towards the grounds of **Failand House**. The Fry residence faces north towards Bristol.

20 Turn right (N) in 400 metres, along **Oxhouse Lane**, to the junction in 500 metres. Here we turn left (W) to return to the church in 150 metres.

8 Wraxall and Tyntesfield

A 6-mile walk encircling the National Trust's time-warp Tyntesfield Estate

Tyntesfield, the epitome of Victorian Gothic bristling with towers and turrets, was always a warm house, with masses of pipes which recycled chimney heat around the bathrooms. Each of its 29 rooms came to the National Trust with contents intact, stuffed with Gibbs family memorabilia and treasures, plus the full kit of servant life downstairs. The time-warp extravaganza is now open to the public, though with timed-tickets and limited parking. This walk is intended to complement your visit — by utilising a network of public rights-of-way that encircle parkland, fields and woods of the 500-acre National Trust property.

Level: 🥾 🥾
Length: 6 miles
Terrain: Starts uphill but otherwise generally level though with several cross-field paths liable to ploughing.
Park & start: In All Saints' Church carpark at the south end of Wraxall Hill, immediately above the junction with the B3130.
Postcode: BS48 1NA
Public transport: Buses from Bristol to Nailsea.
Websites:
www.nationaltrust.org.uk/tyntesfield
www.visionofbritain.org.uk

There are two public houses en route but Wraxall has lost its shops. Veteran post-mistress Martha Pike went on beyond her 90th birthday.

Map labels

1
Sidelands Cottage
2
3 Highridge
4
5
Wraxall
Tyntesfield
14
13
Hazel Farm
12
Flax Bourton Road
Failand
Gable Farm
11
10
Watercress Farm
Ashton Hill Plantation
6
7
Mill Farm
9
8 Gatcombe Mill
April Ash

N
W   E
S

1 Set off from the lych gate, up the hill (N), and pass **Wraxall House** and **Highfield House**. In 300 metres, on the fourth of the sharp bends, we turn right for just 10 metres. Then turn left (E), into the trees, instead of passing **Rectory Cottage**. Bear right in 200 metres into the dense and rocky wood. Emerge in a field in a further 200 metres. Continue straight ahead, with woodland on either side, and pass gentrified **Sidelands Cottage**.

2 Beyond, in 200 metres, we continue straight ahead at a cross-roads of paths. Leave the fields in 400 metres and cross the drive above **Tyntesfield**. Again continue straight ahead, into a narrow gap between stone walls to the left of a

National Trust Tyntesfield

yew tree, with a quarry down to the left. Enter an arable field in 125 metres and continue straight ahead. Follow power cables and keep the **Tyntesfield Park** wall to your right. Cross a stile in 500 metres, down in the corner, beyond the lodge.

3 Bear left (ENE) in this field, up the slope, towards the central clump of trees. Beyond the trees we gradually converge with the road, in 300 metres, and join it at a gate and stile opposite **Highridge**.

Wellingtonia on Ashton Hill

4 Turn right (ESE), facing oncoming traffic and passing **Horse Race Lane**, to descend to the **Failand Inn** in 400 metres. Continue to the crossroads at **Oxhouse Lane** in 200 metres.

5 Turn right (S), beside **Auto Scudia**, into **Flax Bourton Road**. Pass **Jubilee Road** (for George V in 1935). In 900 metres, on reaching the junction on **Belmont Hill** - opposite **Clifton Lodge** - we cross **Weston Road** into the Forestry Commission access road. Enter **Ashton Hill Plantation** and bear right. Continue straight ahead at the junction in 200 metres. Turn right (SW) in a further 400 metres after a stand of tall Pacific coast redwoods (known as Wellingtonia for the Iron Duke). Descend to a tarred road in 50 metres.

6 This drops down to **Kingcot Farm** at the corner in 200 metres. Continue to **Gatcombe Mill House** in a further 400 metres.

Gatcombe valley

Bristol merchant William Gibbs commissioned John Norton to design Tyntesfield in 1863, and Sir Arthur Blomfield to add its Byzantine-style private chapel - covered in mosaics and the biggest in the land - in 1875.

7 Turn right (NW) along a stony drive to the right of the house, and cross a stile beside a gate to pass a second house in 150 metres. Follow the former mill leet across the field to a stile in 175 metres which is 75 metres to the right of the stream. In the scrubby pasture on the other side (SW) we cross quarried hummocks above the stream. Join a sunken track on the far side of the slope, in 200 metres, and turn left. Go down it to a point 50 metres from the stream.

George Abraham Gibbs, who brought home hunting trophies from all over the world, was created Baron Wraxall in 1928, and his son George Richard Lawley Gibbs, the reclusive 2nd Lord Wraxall, died in 2001.

The National Trust bought Tyntesfield in 2002, as a time-warp treasure house of family memorabilia in which it seemed as if everything had been delivered a century before and nothing had ever left the building.

Monolith for Queen Victoria's record reign

8 Here we cross a stile into an arable field and follow its left-hand side for 200 metres. Cross the stream at a humped bridge and cross a field to the right of the houses, to the road beside **April Ash** in 150 metres. Turn right (NE), along the pavement, down to the corner in 160 metres. Follow the main road around the bend to the right to a cross-roads in 100 metres.

Importation of South American guano as fertiliser was the foundation of the Gibbs family fortune that built Tyntesfield, inspiring this doggerel verse in Bristol: 'Mr Gibbs got his dibs, selling the turds of foreign birds.'

9 Turn left (SW), along **Station Road**, to the corner opposite **Mill Farm** in 300 metres. Turn right (NW), through the gate into an arable field, towards the woods above Tyntesfield. Cross the middle of this field and the next with the main road over to the right. From the third field, in 500 metres, the path begins to converge with the road, to reach it road at gates on the other side of the fourth field in a further 500 metres.

10 However, instead of going on it, we turn left (S) and follow the conifer hedge to the left of the drive into **Gable Farm**. Around the corner, in 200 metres, cross a stile into the field. Bear right (W) for 50 metres, to a stile a short distance to the left of the corner of the field. Cross the muddy green lane and enter the field on the other side. Follow the right-hand hedge to the track at **Watercress Farm** in 200 metres.

Watercress Farm time-warp

11 Turn right along the farm road and then left across the stile into the field in 50 metres. Bear right (NW), towards the church tower, to fence-bars in the hedge in 100 metres. Keep heading for the tower, to a gate on to a track, in 200 metres.

12 Turn right and then left, into the next field, in 30 metres. This is another arable field. Bear right, to the gate in the hedgerow facing you, in 200 metres. Proceed straight ahead across this field to the gate beside **Hazel Farm** in 250 metres.

13 Here we turn right (N), along the farm track, and then up the grassy slope in 50 metres. Bear left on the ridge, above the buildings, to a stile on to the road in 200 metres.

14 Turn left (NW) into Wraxall village. Pass the **Battle Axes Inn** and follow the road to the church-yard in 750 metres.

All Saints' Church

All Saints' Church has a fine Bath stone reredos which is the only one in Somerset to feature the transfiguration of Christ as the Messiah.

9 Brockley and Chelvey

A 7-mile circuit of easy going countryside just a couple of stations from Bristol Temple Meads

This is a railway walk. Nailsea and Backwell Station is midway along the mainline from Bristol Temple Meads to Weston-super-Mare. There are regular stopping trains as well as ample car parking. A nearby lakeland nature reserve is a recent creation.

Nailsea remains hidden behind a bracken-clad ridge and the countryside to the south opens out beyond the railway with clusters of historic hamlets. Just about everything in Chelvey has been there half a millennium, or almost, as Edward Tynte did not build his massive three-storey Manor House until about 1600. Brockley Court and St Nicholas Church are also alone together in the fields.

Level:
Length: 7 miles
Terrain: Easy paths with no serious slopes to spoil things.
Park & start: Beside Backwell Lane, 250 metres north of Nailsea and Backwell Station or come by any stopping train.
Postcode: BS48 1TJ
Public transport: Trains from Bristol Temple Meads and buses from Bristol to Nailsea.
Websites: www.visitchurches.org.uk
www.visionofbritain.org.uk

The church is now cared for by the Churches Conservation Trust. The far point is a field or two away from Claverham Green. Here we turn to head back to the railway and the hill immediately south of Nailsea.

53

1 Set off (S) from the station, towards Backwell, and pass **Backwell Motors**.

2 Turn right (SW) 150 metres after the garage, into **Moor Lane**, and also turn right 150 metres along it, at a narrow junction. This section of lane brings us to a bend in 250 metres.

3 Continue straight ahead (S) over the stile beside the gate. Climb the hill to the stile to the left of the gate in 250 metres. From here we head (SW) to **Grove Farm** and pass to the right of it in 500 metres. Pass the main farmyard and turn right into a cattle track. Then turn left, over a stile in the hedgerow, in 15 metres.

4 Cross a stile to the right of the final barn in 100 metres. Head towards a point a little to the left of the monkey puzzle tree at **Chelvey Water Works**. Go over a stile in 250 metres and cross another pasture. Leave the field at the stile beside the junction in 150 metres.

Deer farm at Chelvey Batch

Chelvey

5 Continue straight ahead into **Chelvey Lane** and pass the pumping station which supplies Bristol. A deer farm covers fields on the other side of the road, towards the woods on Chelvey Batch. Proceed to the next junction in 800 metres.

6 Turn left (S), up the slope and around the corner, to a second junction in 75 metres. Here we bear left, beside **Brockley Elm Farm**, for 50 metres.

7 Turn right (W) opposite the end of the buildings, across a stile into an arable field, and bear left to a stile in the corner in 150 metres. Bear left (SW) in the pasture. Pass to the left of the barns and **Brockley Court**, in 400 metres, where we cross a farm drive and visit **St Nicholas Church** in a further 100 metres.

Brockley

8 Beyond it we follow the farm road (W) to **Littlewood Lane** in 500 metres. Turn right (N) to the road junction after **Littlewood Cottage** in 400 metres.

9 Turn right (E) along **Brockley Way** and pass **Midgell Cottages** and **Stanleaze** in 600 metres.

The Smyth-Piggott family were in residence for 300 years at Brockley Court which claims to have one of the earliest chimneys in England.

10 In 300 metres we turn left (N) across a stile between the sweet chestnuts and oaks of a former drive. Exit from the field in the far left corner in 400 metres. On the other side a grassy track (NW) passes a large pond which is the site of the claypit in **Brickyard Wood**. In 200 metres, after the remains of the brickyard buildings, we continue straight ahead across an arable. There is a hedge to the left and Chelvey hamlet across to the right.

Oaks of an old avenue

(11) In 400 metres we come to a green lane and turn left (W) along it, to the farm road in 150 metres. Turn right (NE), away from **Midgell Farm**, to the junction to the right of the railway bridge in 350 metres. A short diversion into **Chelvey** brings in **St Bridget's Church** and the venerable **Old Hall** and barn - now a showroom for antique beds - in an historic triangle.

Backwell Lake was constructed in 1975, as an emergency pond to take surface water run-off from the newly-built streets of suburban Nailsea, but looks as if it has always been here.

The Old Hall

Passing through Brockley inspired Samuel Taylor Coleridge to round off a poem with the words 'Enchanting spot! O, were my Sara here!'

(12) Our onward route, however, is the other way. Cross the railway (W) and pass the entrance to **Nailsea Court** in 300 metres. Continue straight ahead, around the bend, for 100 metres.

(13) Then turn right, across a stile, and follow the hedgerow (NE). Go through the left-hand gate in 200 metres and pass to the right of **Cherry Orchard Stables** in a further 200 metres. Turn left in **Youngwood Lane** and then right (N) in 40 metres, up the steps to a stile, into the field. Cross another stile to the left of **Bizley Farm** in 150 metres. Bear right in the next pasture to the gate in 100 metres.

14 Continue straight ahead (NE) across the middle of this field to a stile to the left of the barn at **Young Wood Farm** in 300 metres. Also cross the following field, uphill to the stile and gate in the middle of the upper hedgerow in 200 metres.

15 Turn right (E) along a muddy green lane to an oak tree in 400 metres. Beyond it, in 50 metres, we bear right and descend towards **White Oak House**. On leaving this scrubby slope, in holly bushes to our left in 150 metres, we turn right (S) across a stile. We are now in a big pasture and pass a pond. Join **Youngwood Lane**, opposite the barn, in 500 metres.

Nailsea and Backwell Station

16 Turn left, for 35 metres, and then right into the field to the left of the barn. Cross the paddocks (SE), over stiles, down to the lower meadows in 500 metres. Here we bear left, across a footbridge, to the left of an isolated house. Cross this marshy meadow diagonally to the gate below the railway embankment in 175 metres. Turn left (ENE), along **Station Close**, to return to **Nailsea and Backwell Station** in 600 metres. **Backwell Lake** is also this side of the tracks, to the left.

10 Stanton Drew and Pensford

A 6-mile walk through history from prehistoric sacred sites to colliery tips

Level: 🐾 🐾
Length: 6 miles
Terrain: Negotiable paths and no real hills but expect damp patches persisting for much of the year.
Park & start: Turn off the B3130, east of Chew Magna into Stanton Drew village.
Start ref.: ST 597 632
Postcode: BS39 4ES
Public transport: Buses from Bristol to Chew Magna.
Websites:
www.english-heritage.org.uk/stantondrew
www.publow-with-pensford.pc.gov.uk

Stanton Drew Stone Circles are the 'Great Western Temple' of the Bronze Age. These alignments and settings date from 2,100 BC. They overlie an earlier Woodhenge, of great posts raised in concentric circles inside a huge ditch and bank, from 3,000 BC. Somerset's premier ancient monument can be used as a calendar for fixing the Sun's turning points of the year at midsummer sunrise and midwinter sunset. The walk also crosses the Somerset coalfield, where half a century after closure the colliery sites are covered with undergrowth, slag heaps by trees, and rail lines reclaimed by pastures and the plough. Pensford's great monuments are the railway viaduct arches that form its dramatic backdrop and dwarf the 14th-century tower of St Thomas Becket Church. Despite closure of the line and the coal pits it served, Pensford remains distinctly industrial, with miners' cottages and their social club.

Byemills Farm
Pensford
River Chew
13
12
Stone Circles
14
Viaduct
11
Stanton
Drew
16
15
Brook
Cottage
10
Old Colliery
9
8
Whitley
Batts
7
The
Crescent
2
Twinway
Farm
4
6
3
Old
Colliery
Stanton Wick
5
Bromley Farm

The Cove

1. Set off along the road (S) beside the **Druids' Arms** and divert up the steps to the beer garden to see the **Cove** setting of three huge stones. Recent investigation has revealed underground evidence of a Neolithic long barrow burial mound between here and the church. Continue straight ahead at the Upper Stanton junction, in 500 metres, up **Bromley Road**. Pass **Auden House** and continue to **The Drive** in 600 metres.

2. Turn left (E), across a stile in 75 metres, opposite No. 7 **The Crescent**. Follow the hedgerow straight ahead and skirt the left side of **Twinway Farm** in 200 metres. A second public path then turns right (S). Follow the farm track to the end

of the Dutch barn and join a dirt track into the fields. Bear right, keeping the hedgerow to your right, to a gate near the corner of the field in 350 metres. This point is opposite the entrance to Curls Farm.

3 Turn left (SE) along the road to **Bromley Farm** in 250 metres. Turn left and then right into the farmyard. Cross it diagonally to the left of the stone outbuilding on triple arches. Turn right (NE) in the field in 50 metres, keeping the hedge to your right, and cross the stile beside the ditch in 100 metres. There are three paths from here. Ours is straight ahead, down to the left-hand side of the tree-covered slag heap in 150 metres. The coal mine was further across to the right.

4 Here there are two paths and ours is again straight ahead. In 150 metres we turn left, across a footbridge over a ditch, and then right in the field. Follow the dense hedgerow. In 75 metres we turn right (E) across a stream and stile. Proceed straight ahead, upwards, to the stile in the corner in 200 metres.

Stone alignment angles from 2100 BC have now shifted eastwards at sunrise (further away from north) and at sunset (towards north) due to the wobble of the Earth's spin - or precession and obliquity of the ecliptic as the 26,000-year cycle is known.

Pensford Viaduct carried a branch line of the Great Western Railway, from Bristol to Midsomer Norton, which closed on 15 July 1968.

5 Continue straight ahead (SE) across the next field to a stile on the other side in 150 metres. Cross traces of a tramway which ran from the colliery to the railway. Follow the next hedge to a stile in the fence beneath the power line near the top of the hill in 200 metres. Bear left (E) to the closest cottage in **Stanton Wick** hamlet. Exit from the field in 250 metres, over a stile to the right of the gate, between the houses and the bungalows.

Great Circle

6 Turn left (N) along the road and follow it to the right (NE) in 50 metres at **Keppelgate** which has an idiosyncratic cottage with a curving back wall. Pass the **Carpenters' Arms** and go over the hill at **Parsons Farm** to the corner in 600 metres.

7 Turn right, across a stile in the hedge, 20 metres before the field gate. Turn left on the other side and keep the hedge to your left. Proceed straight ahead for 500 metres and cross **Salter's Brook**. Another old colliery is in woodland to the left.

8 Turn left through the under-growth and then right, up the slope for 100 metres, and cross the causeway of a disused railway in 100 metres. Follow the conifer hedge and wall to emerge on the A37 beside **Pensford House** at **Whitley Batts** in 150 metres.

9 Cross the main road into **Birchwood Lane**. In the dip in 200 metres we turn left across a stile immediately before the drive to **Sandhills**. Follow the hedgerow straight ahead (N) to a farm track in 200 metres. This goes over the hill towards the village. Bear left (NW) in 200 metres to the road in 100 metres.

10 Turn right (NNW) down **Pensford Old Road** which used to be the main road into Pensford. It becomes the **High Street** and passes former miners' cottages with a pebbled raised pavement beside the **Old Bakery** in 800 metres. Next is **Green's Folly**, dated 1782, followed by the imposing **George and Dragon**. A beehive-shaped **Lock-up** is beside the junction.

Viaduct backdrop

11 From here we turn left (W), down to the modern main road, and cross into **Church Street**. Spot the 'Flood Level' of 10 July 1968, ten feet up at the top of a downstairs window opposite the **War Memorial**. Approach the offending **River Chew**. Eighteenth-century **Bridge House**, to the left in 50 metres, has Salter's Brook beneath it.

Pensford Lock-up

12 Turn left here and then immediately right to pass **Sally Higgins Cottage**. Turn right (NW) opposite the farm in 100 metres, through a kissing gate, and go under the riverside arch of **Pensford Viaduct**. Look up for that reverse-vertigo sensation.

(13) Follow the River Chew and keep it to your right. Continue straight ahead in the following field as the river bends further away. The path is closer to the river in the next field as we approach **Byemills Farm** in 750 metres. Pass to the left of it and then proceed straight ahead (SW) across a stile, into the field facing you.

(14) Cross stiles in the next field with the river to your right. Then cross higher ground, beside an ash tree, to follow power cables. Then a hedge brings us to **Upper Stanton Drew** in 750 metres. Cross the road to the right of a Gothic-arched packhorse bridge below **Brook Cottage**.

(15) Enter the arable field and follow its right-hand hedgerow. Cross the next road in 250 metres, into a fruit field, to head (W) for the church tower. Cross a stile in the dense hedgerow in 250 metres (40 metres to the left of the power line). Again head for the tower. Cross the stile beside the gate and walk up the slope to the farm road in the top right-hand corner of the field in 350 metres. Cross the stiles beside its gates.

(16) There is a view from the next corner, in 100 metres, of **Stanton Drew Stone Circles**. The Great Circle is in the foreground, and the North Eastern Circle beyond it, with a short avenue of big stones linking the two. The South Western Circle is up on the rise to the left and has a view across to the church and over the valley. To visit them, turn right at the farm and walk down to Court Farm House, then follow signs (for a pay path rather than a public one). Or continue straight ahead into the village, in 200 metres, via a short diversion to see **St Mary's Church**.

North Eastern Circle